ALL ABOUT ARACHNIDS
TRAPDOOR SPIDERS

by Becca Becker

pogo

Ideas for Parents and Teachers

Pogo Books let children practice reading informational text while introducing them to nonfiction features such as headings, labels, sidebars, maps, and diagrams, as well as a table of contents, glossary, and index.

Carefully leveled text with a strong photo match offers early fluent readers the support they need to succeed.

Before Reading

- "Walk" through the book and point out the various nonfiction features. Ask the student what purpose each feature serves.
- Look at the glossary together. Read and discuss the words.

Read the Book

- Have the child read the book independently.
- Invite them to list questions that arise from reading.

After Reading

- Discuss the child's questions. Talk about how they might find answers to those questions.
- Prompt the child to think more. Ask: Did you know about trapdoor spiders before reading this book? What more would you like to learn about them?

Pogo Books are published by Jump!
5357 Penn Avenue South
Minneapolis, MN 55419
www.jumplibrary.com

Copyright © 2025 Jump!
International copyright reserved in all countries.
No part of this book may be reproduced in any form without written permission from the publisher.

Library of Congress Cataloging-in-Publication Data

Names: Becker, Becca, author.
Title: Trapdoor spiders / by Becca Becker.
Description: Minneapolis, MN: Jump!, Inc., [2025]
Series: All about arachnids | Includes index.
Audience: Ages 7-10
Identifiers: LCCN 2024037480 (print)
LCCN 2024037481 (ebook)
ISBN 9798892136242 (hardcover)
ISBN 9798892136259 (paperback)
ISBN 9798892136266 (ebook)
Subjects: LCSH: Trap-door spiders—Juvenile literature.
Classification: LCC QL458.42.C83 B43 2025 (print)
LCC QL458.42.C83 (ebook)
DDC 595.4/4—dc23/eng/20241021
LC record available at https://lccn.loc.gov/2024037480
LC ebook record available at https://lccn.loc.gov/2024037481

Editor: Katie Chanez
Designer: Emma Almgren-Bersie

Photo Credits: Wacpan/Dreamstime, cover; RealityImages/Shutterstock, 1; Timothy Cota/iStock, 3, 23; Panlrob Samsuwan/iStock, 4; James H. Robinson/Science Source, 5; antasfoto/Adobe Stock, 6-7; Dr. Paul Zahl/Science Source, 8-9; Mohd Zaidi Razak/Alamy, 10; Federico.Crovetto/Shutterstock, 11, 14-15; Nature Picture Library/Alamy, 12-13; Jason E. Bond and Rebecca L. Godwin/Wikimedia, 16; Nelson Ferretti, Gabriel Pompozzi, Pedro Cardoso/Wikimedia, 17; Pong Wira/Shutterstock, 18-19; Pichit Sansupa/Shutterstock, 20-21.

Printed in the United States of America at Corporate Graphics in North Mankato, Minnesota.

TABLE OF CONTENTS

CHAPTER 1
Digging Burrows 4

CHAPTER 2
Building Trapdoors 10

CHAPTER 3
Growing Up 16

ACTIVITIES & TOOLS
Try This! 22
Glossary 23
Index 24
To Learn More 24

CHAPTER 1

DIGGING BURROWS

An insect crawls on the forest floor. A predator hides. It waits for the insect to come closer.

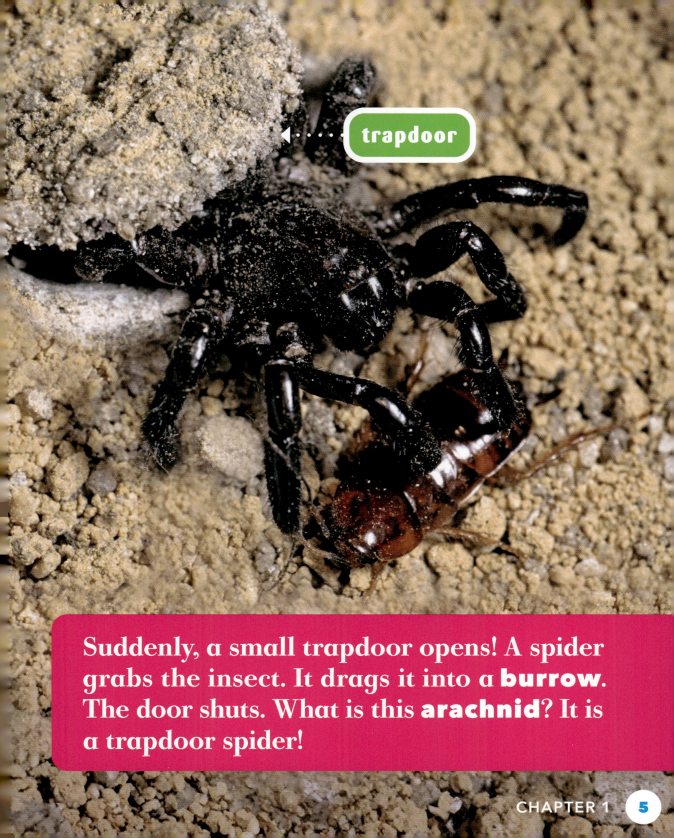

trapdoor

Suddenly, a small trapdoor opens! A spider grabs the insect. It drags it into a **burrow**. The door shuts. What is this **arachnid**? It is a trapdoor spider!

Trapdoor spiders dig burrows in the ground. They dig with their **chelicerae**. Then they roll the dirt into a ball. They use their strong back legs to kick the dirt ball away.

CHAPTER 1

TAKE A LOOK!

What are the parts of a trapdoor spider? Take a look!

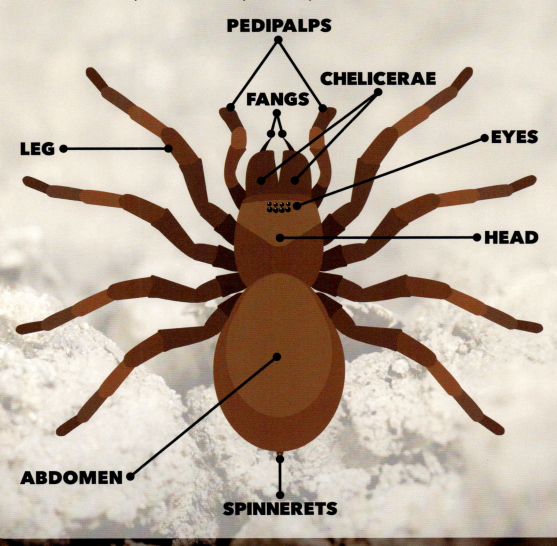

CHAPTER 1   7

Some dig burrows up to 16 inches (40 centimeters) deep. Trapdoor spiders spend a lot of time in their burrows. Why? They are safe inside. It is hard for predators to reach them. They are safe from bad weather, too.

DID YOU KNOW?

Trapdoor spiders live all around the world. They live where they can dig into the ground to make their homes. This includes forests and deserts.

CHAPTER 1

CHAPTER 2
BUILDING TRAPDOORS

Some trapdoor spiders make a door for their burrow. They build the door with materials like dirt, silk, leaves, and moss. The trapdoor is **camouflaged**. It is hard to see! Spiders spin silk to make a **hinge**.

trapdoor

If a predator finds the burrow, the spider stays inside. It bites the trapdoor. Why? This holds it shut. The predator cannot get in!

CHAPTER 2

When **prey** comes close to the burrow, the spider feels the **vibrations**. It quickly opens the trapdoor. It grabs the insect! It brings it inside the burrow to eat. Trapdoor spiders eat insects like beetles, crickets, and grasshoppers.

DID YOU KNOW?

Trapdoor spiders are **nocturnal**. They hunt at night.

CHAPTER 2

Spiders cannot chew. How do they eat? The trapdoor spider bites prey with its fangs. **Venom** goes into the prey. Its insides turn to liquid! The spider sucks it up.

CHAPTER 2

CHAPTER 3
GROWING UP

Females spend most of their lives in or near their burrows. Males go out to look for females to **mate** with.

male

female

16 CHAPTER 3

After mating, a female lays eggs inside her burrow. She wraps them in a silk egg sac. She attaches the egg sac to the wall. She guards it.

egg sac

CHAPTER 3

Spiderlings hatch. They stay in the burrow for months. Each spiderling has a hard **exoskeleton**. As the spiderling ages, its body grows too big for the exoskeleton. The spiderling **molts**. It sheds the exoskeleton. It grows a new one that fits.

CHAPTER 3

Spiderlings leave the burrow when they are big enough to live on their own. They look for a good spot to dig their own burrows. Some will make trapdoors, too!

> ### DID YOU KNOW?
>
> Trapdoor spiders make their burrows wider as they grow. Why? So they can fit!

CHAPTER 3

ACTIVITIES & TOOLS

TRY THIS!

BUILD A HOME

Trapdoor spiders dig burrows. This is their home. Make your own home with this fun activity!

What You Need:
- a cardboard box big enough to fit inside
- scissors
- markers

❶ Use the scissors to cut open a door in the box. You can cut out a window, too. Ask an adult if you need help.

❷ Use markers to decorate your box.

❸ Go inside your box. How do you feel inside? How do you think a trapdoor spider feels inside its burrow?

GLOSSARY

arachnid: A creature with a body divided into two parts, such as a spider or a scorpion.

burrow: A tunnel or hole in the ground used as an animal home.

camouflaged: Hidden or disguised.

chelicerae: Jaws arachnids have that hold prey.

exoskeleton: A hard protective or supporting structure on the outside of an arachnid's body.

hinge: A joint on a door that allows it to open and close easily.

insect: A small animal with three pairs of legs, one or two pairs of wings, and three main body parts.

mate: To come together to produce babies.

molts: Sheds an outer layer.

nocturnal: Active at night.

predator: An animal that hunts other animals for food.

prey: Animals hunted by other animals for food.

spiderlings: Baby spiders.

venom: Poison.

vibrations: Trembling motions.

ACTIVITIES & TOOLS   23

INDEX

burrow 5, 6, 8, 10, 11, 13, 16, 17, 19, 20
camouflaged 10
chelicerae 6, 7
dig 6, 8, 20
eggs 17
egg sac 17
exoskeleton 19
fangs 7, 14
hinge 10
insect 4, 5, 13

mate 16, 17
molts 19
nocturnal 13
predator 4, 8, 11
prey 13, 14
silk 10, 17
spiderlings 19, 20
trapdoor 5, 10, 11, 13, 20
venom 14
vibrations 13

TO LEARN MORE

Finding more information is as easy as 1, 2, 3.

1. Go to www.factsurfer.com
2. Enter "trapdoorspiders" into the search box.
3. Choose your book to see a list of websites.